To: Tess
From: Meralda
10/27/21

All the King's Horses

by

Maureen Doyle

with Barbara van den Akker

DORRANCE
PUBLISHING CO
EST. 1920
PITTSBURGH, PENNSYLVANIA 15238

Dorrance Publishing Co
585 Alpha Drive
Pittsburgh, PA 15238
Visit our website at *www.dorrancebookstore.com*

ISBN: 978-1-6461-0477-2
eISBN: 978-1-6461-0717-9

To my children, Anne-Marie, Scott, and Donnie,
with love and thanks.

Introduction

When Maureen asked me to introduce her book I was delighted. I have known her for over 35 years and have witnessed what I esteem to be Christianity lived out the way the Lord meant it to be. Just recently in the saddest trial of her life, she exhibited the reality of living in God's Rest. The Rest spoken of in Hebrews 4 is real. It is a real Place and it is a real Person.

Before I was born again, I was a very religious person. If the doors to the church were open, I was there. But I was not born again, and I deeply resented it when others tried to tell me so. I didn't understand what they meant about the difference between religion and relationship until Jesus revealed Himself to me.

I think Rest is like that. After we are born again, we can think because we have a newfound peace, we have that Rest. But we do not. It is not until we stop trying to live the Christian life and simply learn to live with Jesus 24/7 in our hearts and minds that we enter into this Place unlike any other.

It is a Place where we come to trust God no matter what life holds for us. It is where we can relate to the apostle Paul when he says that he had learned whatsoever state he was in therein to be content. Rest is where we realize that religion can't give us what we need. Keeping every law there is cannot bring us into this amazing Place. It is only by abandoning SELF and via Obedience Street and Trust Road, allowing Jesus in us to live His life through us, that we enter into this Rest.

It is a Place of peace and comfort of soul and (forgive me) giddiness. It is a place where you know that God's plan really is better than your own. It is also a very hard-traveled journey. There really are floods and fires and raging winds with drenching rains. There are deep, dark valleys and steep treacherous mountains. It is a lonely path. It is also the ONLY way to the City of Sabbath Rest. It is a Place where once reached we wonder – what took us so long?

I am blessed and delighted to write this introduction to Maureen's story because I have been with her and seen her time and time again do the necessary spiritual battle to overcome her flesh (mind, will, and emotions). She has weathered the journey and entered the gates of the City. NO small task.

It is my prayer that as you read this testimony you will look beyond the words and see the truth of their message. I pray you will discover the wonder of falling into the Arms you cannot see trusting they are there and though yet unseen being totally upheld and kept safe and secure within them… because Sabbath Rest is not only a Place it is The Lord Jesus Christ. Maureen has entered and I pray you do, too. Jesus waits with arms open wide to receive you.

Barbara van den Akker

Foreword

I have written that the reader will find hope in realizing that no matter the mess one makes of their life, God is able to transform that mess into a life worth living. He has taken me from emotional prison to emotional freedom, and that freedom is worth the pain of whatever we have to give up in the process: unforgiveness, fear, anger, self-pity, pride, lust, finances, family, friendships, or perhaps a job, a place of residence, or even a civic or social organization. God restores broken relationships and gives us His peace, love, and joy along with confident assurance of who we are in Christ and who Christ is in us.

What He has done for me He will do for anyone who turns to Him with a humble and contrite heart.

Know you are not alone. He will make you into an overcomer and more than a conqueror of your soul.

I want others to experience the same freedom walking with God has occasioned in me. To that end, you are in my prayers.

All scriptures are from the King James Version of the Bible.

Maureen Doyle

Easton, Massachusetts 2019

Part One

The Lost Is Found

Firstborn to Marie and Leo Lynch was their Maureen at South Shore Hospital, South Weymouth, Massachusetts, on August 28, 1943. We lived for a short time in East Weymouth next door to neighbors who became life-long friends.

When I was one, we moved to a federal housing project into a two-family on Hemlock Road in Hingham. In those days, families interacted with each other around kitchen tables. Children played games inside and out. Television didn't enter homes until the 50's (black and white, of course). Our home was heated by a coal stove in the basement. That demanded coal to be shoveled daily; and yes, even I shoveled coal when old enough.

Though I can hardly believe it, at age four my mother would put me on a train at South Station in Boston. Mom would tell the conductor to keep an eye on me, and that my nana would meet me at the other end in Worcester. My brother, Paul, three at the time, accompanied me at times. This probably couldn't happen in today's embattled and unsafe society.

My nana was my lifeline and my escape from home life. I was too young to understand the reason why, but only knew that my mother's yelling and my father's drinking made me want to run away.

I loved spending time with my nana. She gave me many happy memories: taking me to White City Amusement Park in Shrewsbury, to the beach, and to have an ice cream (still today my favorite comfort treat). Nana also took me shopping to The Mart. Again, shopping remains another of my comfort zones.

I thank God for giving me my nana but have had to ask His forgiveness for allowing those precious held memories to lead me into bondage, which I address later in my story.

At that same time in our lives, Paul and I went out to play before noon on Sunday, March 7, 1948, with instructions from our mother not to go near the pond about 100 yards from our home. We went with two neighbor kids: a girl, age five and her brother, age three. The pond (which was a drainage pond) was frozen except for an area where the embankment had a pipe below where water poured in. Paul was sitting near the edge of the embankment and started to get up. I reached out to stop him from standing, but he slipped and fell into the icy cold water.

The other children and I tried to fish him out with sticks, but with no success. We ran to my home crying to my mother that Paul was in the water. My mother ran to the scene while screaming for help. What ensued was great commotion. Two neighbors who lived near the pond were the first to arrive. Paul was floating face down. One man jumped in, grabbing and pulling him out. He and another man gave him mouth to mouth for 15 minutes before the Hingham Fire Department arrived. Two doctors and a priest also arrived. The firemen worked on Paul for over an hour with an inhalator, using three oxygen tanks. Medical aid was also administered and finally Paul was pronounced dead by accidental drowning.

When I began thinking about writing this story, I obtained a copy of Paul's death certificate and went to the Hingham Library to obtain a copy of the newspaper account of Paul's drowning. Sitting in the parking lot, reading it and crying and crying and crying, I called my sister, Melanie, and read it to her.

Mel commented, "Is that the reason I am mentally challenged?" She was not joking. At the time of Paul's drowning, our mother was pregnant with her. Melanie said mentally, but really she meant emotionally. She was very close to our mom, so when Ma died many years later, Melanie collapsed emotionally.

With this new information about Paul's drowning, I discovered that several months earlier our Dad had saved a four-year-old boy who had fallen through the ice on his scooter at this very pond.

On February 22, 1948, a few weeks before Paul's drowning, a three-year-old girl was saved from drowning there also. My Dad had saved the boy and knew about the girl's rescue, but he wasn't able to save his own three-year-old son. In all those years, I had never heard this story. Dad was a hero. My eyes were now opened regarding my Dad and his probable reason for drinking. That knowledge helped me relinquish some of the hate I had held against him. I have forgiven him and asked God to forgive me for holding onto unforgiveness. That release brought a freedom and lightness to my heart.

The guilt of not following my mother's warning of the pond became, at that young age, a lump of guilt in my chest. With each memory of Paul's drowning and my own disobedience, it grew larger. I was the eldest at four. Paul was three. The burden of guilt in me was lifted somewhat when an Episcopal priest with whom I shared this many years later said that at the age of four, I could not be held responsible. Even though that dear man said those words, they only brought temporary comfort, for later in life I realized that I was responsible for my sin of disobedience.

On January 8, 2018, 69 years after this incident, I was riding with my friend, Barbi, in her car and she asked me about ice-skating as we saw some people skating. I told her I didn't skate because of the drowning incident of my brother. We were almost to her house in Marshfield when she suggested we go to the scene where it happened in Hingham at least 40 minutes away to pray. It occurred to us that there was more to be set free in me regarding this incident. We turned around and headed for the pond in Hingham where we sat and prayed. As we did, God brought much of what had happened back to my mind. Guilt had stuffed hurtful memories deep inside of me. Guilt had paralyzed me. We prayed for the other children, their parents, those who tried but couldn't save Paul, and neighbors who had witnessed this devastating scene and how their lives might have been affected.

As before mentioned, at the time of Paul's drowning, my mother was pregnant with Melanie and my brother, Michael, was one. Michael told me many years later that he felt sad because he didn't have a chance to get to know Paul and play with him.

As Barbi and I sat praying that day, I also shared a story with her about a time Joe, my recently deceased husband, and I were watching Stefano, Sofia, and Sandro (three of our shared grandchildren) at our home in East Bridgewater. Joe was letting them walk out into the wetlands, parts of which were dry, behind our home to explore. He was watching them very carefully, but I was in a panic the whole time, and Joe encouraged me not to worry. I did not understand why these feelings were choking me until God revealed to me the memory of my brother's drowning and those emotions that were hidden for so many years had come to light. That horrific drowning many years prior was the cause of my reacting in panic mode.

It is God's job to reveal the hidden things, and this was a big one for me. God did a wonderful inner healing in me the day Barbi and I were at the pond because we obeyed the leading of His Holy Spirit and returned to the scene.

• • •

> A word of caution:
> Be aware and beware of the words we speak to others, for unknowingly we could be putting guilt

and/or our responsibility off onto them no matter their age.

No amount of psychoanalysis or counseling could have done the healing work God did in me that January 2018 day in just one hour.

• • •

Now I am free to say goodbye to Paul; to receive God's forgiveness, made possible when I forgave the others involved; and to understand that guilt from Paul's death was the reason I rebelled against responsibility in later life. Now I am able and willing to assume responsibilities with a right-heart attitude, and I have learned that all responsibilities must be of God's choosing and not my own. I lived with much fear that something would happen on my watch, causing an added burden of guilt. These many years later, how sweet is the freedom only God was able to give deep within my heart…in His time and in His way. Ecclesiastes 3:11 tells us that He makes all things beautiful in HIS time.

On March 13, 1953, when I was 10 years old, my youngest sister, Marilyn, was born. Shortly thereafter she developed triple pneumonia. I am so glad she came through that time in her life. To this day we still call her "the baby."

Several months after God began this healing work from Paul's death, in August of 2018, I drove alone to the neighborhood where I spent the first 12 years of my life. I drove around the neighborhood and remembered other things that obviously affected my later sexual life.

A neighbor (an adult family friend at that time) would have me sit on his lap and he would experience an erection. I was too young to know what was happening, but subconsciously it registered.

A second thing that came to mind was when two older boys from the neighborhood took me to the woods and made me do something sexual to them. I was very naïve but again, it registered.

I also remembered going to a sleepover at a family friend's home. I shared my girlfriend's bed. Her father came in and tried to reach inside the top of my nightgown. I was very frightened and knew that this was not right. I kept moving around trying not to let him know I was awake, hoping to stop what he was attempting to do. He eventually did stop and left the room. Shame and fear kept me from telling anyone. Though I never said anything about those incidents, I am sure they affected my later sexual life.

• • •

> Please, if something like this has or is happening to you, TELL SOMEONE.

• • •

At age 12, my parents moved to Polk Road still in Hingham. Somewhere between the ages of 13 and 14, I worked on a farm one street over from where we lived. Work consisted of milking cows, cleaning the manure troughs, driving the tractor to spread manure, making bales of hay and throwing them on a truck, then stacking them in the barn. One of the male owners molested me (hands only) while I was sitting on the bales of hay in the barn, and again I didn't tell anyone. However, this time, I kept going back and letting it continue, as it felt good. Shame and fear existed that I would be exposed because of going back, but I let it continue. Somewhere inside of me, I had to know this was wrong. I believe these occurrences were the start of my search for love and acceptance through physical pleasure in all the wrong places.

It is important that you know that I have since forgiven all those men and boys. Just as important, I have also forgiven myself and God for allowing this to happen.

It has been said that God permits what He hates to accomplish what He loves. He loves me, and my wholeness and freedom were what He was in the process of accomplishing.

At some point during those young teen years, my nana told me that my father was out with some blonde while I was being born. True or not, it added to the hatred I had toward my father and I took his absence as rejection. I'm sure he loved me, but I held onto that part of the hate for many years until I attended a Christian retreat in 1982. As I confessed my sin of hatred before God, He graciously delivered me. I was filled with God's joy unspeakable and full of glory. Laughter poured out of me and was definitely the medicine I needed. Thank You, Lord Jesus. You are the Healer and Lover of my soul. When I cooperate with You, You bring freedom and joy with Your forgiveness.

While at Hingham High School, I joined every-after school sport so I wouldn't have to go home (softball, field hockey, basketball, and archery). Home was not where I wanted to spend my time as it stirred up so many negative emotions - not to mention other responsibilities that came with being the oldest.

My dad's drinking problem affected the whole family. He drank at home and at a local bar. My mother would pick him up as he had lost his license. She would pack the three of us (Marilyn had not yet been born) in the car and we would go park in front of the bar and wait and wait and wait and wait until he would be ready to go home.

Riding home from that bar one evening, my mother was driving, and the back door of the car opened. My brother, Michael, then three years old, fell out. As a result of that fall, he was diagnosed with epilepsy, and they said it could have happened from hitting his head. My mother said I should have made sure the door was shut, adding to my growing guilt. I was seven years old. Even as I type this, I forgive you again, Mom; and I ask You again, Father God, to forgive me for holding on to it.

Receiving my license at 16 meant the responsibility of picking my father up at the bar now fell on me. I would take my friend, Ethel, with me and we would wait and wait and wait and wait. At times Ethel and I would go and hang out in the upper square in East Weymouth while we waited. We would drive back to the bar to see if my father was ready to go home. He would keep coming to the door and putting up one finger which meant either one more drink or one more minute (which was usually not one more minute) until he finally came out. If he didn't come out, we would go back to the upper square drug store where kids usually hung out and hang around until Dad was ready to go home.

Now anger was joining guilt as fully grown plants in my heart and mind.

I thank God that there are some good memories of my Dad. I remember a fun family time when we would go to Nantasket Beach for steamed hot dogs on a steamed roll with mustard, relish, and onions. Mmmmmmmmm. The best. Later in my story, I'll share others.

During high school years, Ethel and I hung out. One day we were invited to a boy's house with other boys and girls, not knowing that we were to watch pornographic films in the basement room. We watched for a short time, and realizing it was wrong, we left. However, watching them fueled the growing sexual appetite in me.

Illicit sex took hold, and over the years, I allowed things to be done to me that were perverted. I also did perverted things to myself. Do not believe the mistaken idea this happens only to men. The tentacles reach women, too, and it totally affects the thought life and all sin starts in our thought life.

God has delivered and healed me, but I will *always* have to be careful what I listen to, what I watch, and what I read because the possibility of reopening a closed door to demonic sexual activity is always present. I will always have to do battle fighting the thoughts when they come by using spiritual weapons I have learned from the Bible. In His Word, God has given us all we need to have spiritual victory. Different weapons will work for different people. Each of us must learn what works for us to stay pure before God. As we learn to listen and obey the Holy Spirit, using His weapons will become second nature to us. Weapons such as praise, forcing thoughts captive, meditating on God's Word, etc. So you see, God's weapons bring life and healing to our damaged souls where the world's weapons bring destruction.

I am to be led by the Holy Spirit, obeying whatever He puts on my heart for the current battle to keep myself pure. It is a lifelong battle and though I falter, faltering becomes less as I continue to surrender to God and use the weapons He provides. Choosing to use His weapons (forgiveness, a thankful heart, praise, bringing my thoughts captive always back to Jesus...) is my responsibility. God has given each of us the gift of choosing what we will think. We cannot blame anyone else if we dwell on what we consider an offense or a wrong done to us. That kind of thinking is Satan's playground.

• • •

> Yes, the battle ensues. Choices matter. 1 Corinthians 6:18-20 tells us to flee (run from) fornication (sexual sin). Therefore fleeing, or running from, is also a weapon. If we are born again, we are bought with a price, the precious Blood of Jesus. Our

bodies are the home of the Living God and we are to glorify Him by living accordingly.

• • •

When I was a high school senior, my mother left my father, took my siblings, and went to live in Worcester with her mother, my nana. Because I was a senior, she left me home with my father until my graduation. It was more than I could bear because of his drinking, and he was miserable without her.

Ethel and I connived a way to get her to come home. We drove to Worcester and told her my dad wanted her to come home. We lied; but she came home, making my life easier. Believe it or not Mom and Dad stayed together. Dad eventually stopped drinking, and they were relatively happy until Dad died after 42 years of marriage.

While in high school, another friend moved to Whitman, and Ethel and I would drive there and hang out with her in downtown Whitman. This is where I met a boy we will call C. We dated for a total of three years. At one point in our relationship, I was having extensive work done on my teeth at Tufts Dental School in Boston, and borrowed C's car. On the drive home, the rain was heavy and the road slippery. I remember the car skidding and spinning around. I remember sliding into the guardrail and hitting my head on the steering wheel. The car ricocheted across the highway, stopping in the opposite direction. Looking back, I can see God's protection in that there was either no oncoming traffic or they were able to miss me completely. This happened at the Union Street exit in Braintree. C's car was totaled. Except for hitting my head on the steering wheel and developing a black eye, there were no other physical injuries. But I must have been an emotional wreck as I really don't remember what happened next. There had to be police. There had to be ambulance.

There had to be hospital. There had to be calls to C and my family. They are all gone from my memory.

C and I continued dating. I graduated and started working at the First National Bank in Boston.

Life continued. At one point in our relationship, because my father didn't approve of C, we pretended to break up. I had a friend of his pick me up so I could go and meet him.

On August 6, 1963, my mother received a call from the hospital in Worcester saying that my nana was there and very ill. If we wanted to see her, we should come as soon as possible. My father was working. My mother and I were distraught. My first thought was to call C and ask him to drive us to the Worcester hospital. He did. We arrived but were too late to see my nana. She had died.

I don't remember what happened next until there was a wake (my first at 19 years old). My mother and other relatives were forcing me to go from the room where I was sitting to where the casket was, impressing on me it was the proper thing to do. I was uncontrollably carrying on against it and was an emotional mess; but was forced until I went in. My nana was my rock. All school vacations, summers, and holidays I would spend in Worcester with her. She would take me to White City in Shrewsbury, shopping at The Mart in Worcester, and Filene's Basement in Boston. She would have me try clothes on between the racks. Embarrassing, but I did it. She even took me to New Hampshire so she could play bingo in a big hall as I watched. Now my nana was forever gone.

Eventually C and I were openly back together and engaged to be married. My father was always accusing me of going all the way with C. We didn't. My father's accusations angered me, and, coupled with the fact of our love, his accusations after a year and a half finally became truth.

C and I agreed to marry by a Justice of the Peace because my religion was engrained in me, and I was taught I couldn't marry in or even enter another church. Now my father accepted the fact that we would marry, pushing so much he even offered $1,000 if we would get married in the Catholic church. C told me the Baptist church or not at all. C and I broke up. Recently I have thought about this breakup realizing if we really loved each other, we would have married. Lust is so easily mistaken for love.

Between Nana's death and the chapter of my life with C over, I retreated into my by-then familiar habit pattern of burying reality deep within and living as if nothing was wrong. In writing this out, I am seeing the war that existed between my father and C. It should not have happened. I was old enough to make my own decisions; but allowed that habit pattern of not thinking things through on my own and allowing others to make my decisions to continue as I escaped into my all-too familiar private sanctuary. Of course, all this was adding to my ball of guilt and anger, with fear a close runner up.

I am also realizing that this unhealthy pattern had become a habit for most of my life. When we see things in our early life that we are not emotionally mature enough to either understand or deal with, it is ever so much easier to bury them and to allow others to make decisions for us. Ramifications then become their bailiwick. What a Blame Game quagmire we create.

In my life there was another escape. Soap operas. I watched them all the time and whatever decisions I did make were based on them. When I became a Christian, I stopped watching them because they filled my mind with a false idea of the way life was supposed to be. Life wasn't that way, nor meant to be.

I stopped caring about life in general because I had lost both Nana and C, the only two people I thought really loved me.

I would like to thank my friend, Ethel, because I was unable to attend another wake or funeral until her father died 15 years later. Ethel gently guided me to the casket. I have been able to attend wakes and funerals since.

Also between the time Nana died and C and I broke up, these events together intensified something in me and I stopped caring about my life, stopped caring about anyone. I allowed myself to become emotionally dead. No one did this to me. I did it to myself.

Ethel eventually joined me working at the First National Bank but in a different department. We drove together to Boston, parking in a garage where we met a couple of guys who worked as attendants. After about a year and a half, one of them asked me out. I agreed as we knew them for what seemed like a long enough time.

On our first two dates, we just sat in his car talking. On our third date, he took me to his friend's apartment as he said he had to pick something up. While there, he tried to go all the way. I said "NO!" but he persisted until he overpowered me. Afterward I went to the bathroom, sat on the floor, and cried, knowing something had happened that was different. Sex between C and I, though wrongly timed, was very much consensual. This was not. This was rape. I didn't tell anybody.

One more trauma bludgeoned my heart and I could not wrap my mind around it, so I buried it. It remained deep inside of me until the trauma of writing this book. But this time I had Jesus, and He was revealing the hidden things, cleaning them out and making my soul whole.

• • •

> Today we know when sex is not consensual, it is rape. When it happened to me, I told no one. The emotional trauma of being violated, used, and betrayed made me feel dirty and because there was no ability to become clean on the inside, it was all buried deep within me. I know now that Jesus' love cleanses us on the inside, but that was still in the future.

If something like this has happened to you, PLEASE TELL SOMEONE!

• • •

My life went on. Time passed. Because I no longer cared what happened to me, I allowed myself to continue on the downward spiral of looking for love in wrong places, thus becoming pregnant.

A few months went by when Ethel and I were hanging out in East Weymouth square and heard about a party in town. We went to the house where the party was. At the end of the night, after most others had left, the host of the party came down to the basement room with a loaded gun and started shooting. He fired the first shot, hitting one man in the groin and fired again, hitting another in the arm. Ethel checked to see if they were alright, and we were told to run by the one who had been shot in his arm. We ran in a panic, my heart pounding as I scrambled to the bulkhead, stumbling and fearing for my life to the road where we hid behind her parked car. We had left our jackets and pocketbooks behind. Another man was yelling that there was a maniac in the house with a gun. This brave man, when he had opportunity, went back and retrieved our jackets and pocketbooks. The man toting the gun came out of the house, waving the gun saying he was going to kill us all. There were five of us left at his house. We found out later the gun had five bullets. The police came, and we had to go to the station to answer questions.

Again, life continued, and time passed. One day on our way to work, Ethel and I were talking and in conversation discovered both of us might be pregnant. We were both young with irregular cycles. We decided it was time to go see a doctor. We took a day off from work, randomly stopped at a phone booth, looked in the yellow pages, and just pointed to a doctor in Quincy. We put money in, and rotary dialed, getting appointments together. We continued to work at the bank as long as we could hide the fact of our pregnancies with loose-fitting clothes and girdles. We both kept our second jobs as waitresses. When we could no longer hide our condition, we quit our bank jobs, but pretended to go to work in order to keep the truth from our parents. Instead we spent the day with a friend of ours. This continued for several weeks.

Around that time, a court case from the shooting came up, and we were all summoned as witnesses. Ethel and I went to court in our then very pregnant condition.

We had plans to live in her station wagon and leave town; but our plans were thwarted when my Aunt Kay came from Worcester to Boston and called the bank to have lunch with me and go shopping. To her surprise, she found I no longer worked there. Aunt Kay phoned my mother, telling her of her call to the bank and asking what was happening with me. My mother had no clue.

Ethel and I were going to our bowling league that night in Boston. Before going, I called home. My mother was crying and asked what was wrong. I told her, and she told me to come home and we would work it out.

I let others believe the baby was C's. I wanted the baby to be his because I was embarrassed that I had had sex with someone else and didn't want to have to tell anyone. Deep down inside, I knew the baby wasn't C's but I phoned him and shared it. He denied the baby was his for he knew the timing was off. We never spoke again.

My mother and I did not talk with my father about any of this. He just watched as I grew further and further along in my pregnancy. My mother decided that I was to give the baby up for adoption. At one point, my father said that my baby would not come into his house. I asked my mother many years later why she decided that I was to give up my baby for adoption and said she was afraid of my father's reaction due to one son's drowning and his other son's epilepsy.

Because my family found out about my pregnancy, Ethel chose to tell her family. This meant there would be no running away.

My doctor finally told me to stop my second job waitressing. I had continued waitressing, hiding the pregnancy with an apron. I needed the income. The mess inside of me grew, even as the child inside of me was growing.

While waitressing, I met Donnie. We dated. He knew I was pregnant and told me not to tell anyone, letting others think what they will. However, Donnie had roaming feet and would just take off when he felt the urge, calling me from wherever he went.

The plan was still to give my baby up for adoption. Because of this, I emotionally detached from the baby growing inside. I went to St. Margaret's Hospital in Dorchester for prenatal care and delivery. A social worker at the hospital gave me reasons to keep the baby and reasons to give the baby up. I was confused because I was told the plan for me was adoption. Let me try to explain that at that time in my life, and probably because of my emotional state, I didn't THINK. I just did whatever was put before me. That may be difficult to understand, but for me, it was so.

On August 1, 1964, I delivered a little girl. I had signed a paper refusing to see the baby, but the nurse brought her to me. I thought I had emotionally detached, but I was numb and frightened of holding her. The nurse passed her to me for feeding. I held her at a distance while feeding her and then got up (I was supposed to wait for the nurse) and put her back in the crib.

The day before I was scheduled to go home from the hospital, a miracle happened. Mom and Dad came to visit, and my father stood at the nursery window. He kept repeating, "That's Maureen, that's Maureen all over." They left and later I received a phone call from Mom informing me that my father had given her enough money to buy whatever was needed for me to come home with the baby. A miracle indeed!

She became my Anne-Marie, using my confirmation name, Anne, and my mother's first name, Marie.

Plans were now changed for my life. In hindsight, I see that God knew what needed to be done. I resented the fact that I wasn't given a choice. But neither did I stand up for myself or even think of doing so. I have forgiven and been forgiven of all surrounding that period of my life. Breathe, breathe, breathe.

God wants me whole. In order to be whole, I must be emotionally well. In order to be emotionally well, I must cooperate with the work of the Holy Spirit. His timing. His way. His Plan. The human part of me wants what it wants and wants it now. It doesn't work that way with God. I had been walking with God for at least 13 years before He began to reveal in me hidden things that needed to be dealt with. What was found in there was unforgiveness, anger, fear, sexual perversion, guilt, shame, self-absorption, and resentment along with all of the habit patterns they caused: overeating, addicted to shopping, not facing responsibility, letting people take the lead, depending on television so my mind would not have to think, nor would I be doing anything productive. The revealing and the healing did not happen all at once. God is too gracious for that. It took years and it is still a work in process. God and I are in our 36th year and He is not finished with me yet; otherwise He would take me Home.

I discovered three keys to cooperating with the Holy Spirit as He does His work of making my soul free:

Patience with myself and Him

Trusting Him totally

Obedience to every one of His leadings

The quicker I obey Him, the easier life flows. Not that situations change, but the way I deal with them and think about them changes.

The day Anne-Marie and I came home from the hospital, Donnie showed up at the house. He had been on one of the sporadic, spontaneous trips of his. Obviously, this habit did nothing to enhance our relationship. I was nervous because he didn't know that I had taken my baby home and was not going through with the plan of adoption. When I saw his car pull up, I ran out of the house to the driver's side window before he got out because I was afraid of what he would say. I told him I had taken Anne-Marie home, and asked if he still wanted to come in. He came in and even held her.

After six weeks, I returned to work in Boston at my parents' request. Therefore, my mother became my Anne's primary caregiver. I relinquished this control. I am not very proud of it, but neither did I do anything to prevent its happening. I spent as much time with her as I could. I am writing this with tears because I am so glad that Anne-Marie is here in my family and not with another.

Donnie and I continued dating. Donnie gave me a diamond that I lost one night when I was out clubbing. I was taking it on and off my finger. Engaged and out clubbing. What was I thinking?

Donnie and I lied about being married by a Justice of The Peace and moved into an apartment in North Quincy in December of 1966. I left Anne-Marie with my parents so Donnie and I could see if this was going to work out.

He had a drinking problem and would binge drink. I was working, trying to save money and to make ends meet, but I never knew when he would binge and spend the money I had saved. During this time, I missed my Anne and brought her to live with us, but I returned her to my mother's when I realized I could no longer live with Donnie's drinking.

When Donnie drank, he would become verbally abusive, calling me all sorts of names, telling me no one else would want me. That crushed me, and I would sleep in the bathtub until he sobered up. Why the bathtub instead of the couch? Was I, in my distorted thinking, agreeing with Donnie? Is that why I chose the bathtub over the couch? I finally came to the point of telling Donnie it was over and I was leaving.

That day he was riding to work with his father to the power plant in Sandwich on Cape Cod. On the way to work while crossing the Sagamore Bridge, Donnie had a panic attack and wanted to jump out of the car and off the bridge. He must have said that to his dad, because his dad brought Donnie to his house in Hingham.

From there, Donnie called me. We talked and Donnie pleaded, "You wouldn't leave me now?" I told him I wouldn't, and I thought to myself that he needed me. I stayed with him. He stopped drinking. Without a word to anyone we found a Justice of The Peace and this time were legally married on December 7, 1967.

We realized we could no longer afford the North Quincy apartment, and a friend of Donnie's told us about a small apartment in Weymouth. We moved, bringing Anne with us. However, we were not there more than a few months as it leaked when it rained; but in those few months, Donnie was still having panic attacks. I would have to keep a diaper bag and other supplies at the ready, because when the attacks hit him, we all had to get in the car and leave. Driving seemed to calm him down.

Because our apartment was leaky, we had been looking and found a rental house in Hingham. We moved once again.

Donnie and I were happy in this little house near Hingham bay, but one day, and this was before Anne started school and could not have been more than four, she decided to go exploring outside before Donnie and I woke up. When we realized Anne was not in the house,

I remembered the nearby water and my brother's drowning, and I panicked. But she was safe. We found her but the panic was there still buried deep within me as part of the lumps of guilt and fear.

Donnie decided he would adopt Anne-Marie before she started school and did so on May 14, 1968, so she would have his name when she entered kindergarten that September.

While still in the house at the bay, we became pregnant with Scott. He was born on December 29, 1968. For a while it seemed as though life had straightened out. Donnie had stopped drinking. With Scott's birth I had a girl, a boy, an alcohol-free husband, and now plans for a new home of our own. I thank God that Scott was an easy and enjoyable baby, and now he is a responsible and enjoyable man with a family of his own.

Because we now had two children, we began looking for a larger place. Finding a house in the same area, we decided to move forward and purchase it. The seller kindly let us move in before papers were signed. However, the pressure of the thought of a mortgage must have been too much for Donnie. He changed his mind, and after only 12 days we moved yet again. Thank God the papers had not yet been signed and thank God for an understanding seller.

This time our parents sheltered us. At that time Donnie inherited some money, relieving the pressure of the thought of a mortgage and freeing us to buy a house in Hanover.

This should have been the beginning of a good experience. It was not. Donnie started to drink again. And we were both into things we should not have been. Although this was not a good time in our lives together, we were blessed by becoming pregnant with our second son. Donnie, Jr., was a blessing then and is a blessing now, also with a family of his own.

During this pregnancy, Mom, my sister, Melanie, and I joined a bowling league. One night after rolling the ball at my turn, I felt the unmistakable release of fluid down my legs. I turned and ran to Mom, telling her something was wrong. It was too soon. She took me home, and we called the doctor. He said it was a pretty sure thing I was having a miscarriage and for me to go to bed. He also said that if God wanted this baby born, I'd be okay. I couldn't sleep in our bed because I had gained so much weight in the pregnancy and our mattress was less than to be desired, sagging in the middle. I had trouble getting out, so I slept on the couch. Donnie would sleep on the floor in front of the couch to be with me. This was such a kind and loving act on Donnie's part that even though he had returned to drinking, it was the first time I really believed he loved me.

The doctor was honest with us and gave no guarantee that I would carry to full term. On July 7, 1972, Donnie, Jr., came into the world weighing a whopping 10 lbs., 12 oz. and was 22 inches long. He was not only *not* premature, but I carried him an extra month beyond delivery date also. Obviously, God wanted this baby to be born. Another miracle.

My sister, Marilyn, – then age 18 - was in the waiting room and could hear me screaming in labor. She said she was not having any children, ever. She has since married and had three children and is now the grandmother of two.

Because he had gone back to drinking after being sober for three years, Donnie was not available for support when I was in the hospital.

I had gained a lot of weight during the pregnancy and Donnie blamed me for Donnie, Jr.'s having a pinched nerve in his back, paralyzing him on his left side. He wanted to be held all the time. My arms would feel like they were going to fall off. When anyone came to visit, I would welcome the help. One way he would be calm and go to sleep was when I turned on the vacuum cleaner in the hall outside his room, leaving it running. We were told the paralyzing might or might not heal. Thank God it did when he was three months old.

At nine months, Donnie, needed a cast to straighten his left foot and lower leg. He would walk on the cast and wear it out. I was eventually told to wrap tape around the cast. It worked. Donnie, Jr., walks just fine today at age 46.

Because Donnie started drinking again, I attended a support group with him. I thought I was helping but I wasn't. I was encouraged to go to a different support group to help me cope. I went to my first meeting and had such a wall built around me I thought if anyone touched me, I'm out of here; but no one did.

It was here that I heard for the first time that God loved me. I continued going and would leave Anne (age 10) watching her brothers. I put too much responsibility on her so I could do what I wanted. History repeating itself.

At this point our marital relationship was so strained that we separated in 1974 and divorced in 1976. I didn't really want the divorce, and I wish things had worked out differently, but they didn't. I did phone him asking forgiveness for my part in the breakup of our marriage. Our relationship improved, but we remained divorced.

I met a lady at the support group I continued to attend who asked me what I had always wanted to do. I said I always wanted to become a hairdresser. She encouraged me to pursue it and I did. Thank you, Sue.

I received a grant to go to hairdressing school and Donnie, Jr., attended day care. I graduated from Mansfield Beauty Academy in Quincy in 1977. I worked at Clickers Hair Salon for two years and then opened my own small shop in Hanover in 1979, eventually coming off the welfare system. My father lent me the money to open. Thanks, Dad.

Because of Anne-Marie's great interest in hairdressing, we agreed for her to attend Mansfield Beauty Academy in Quincy with my sister, Marilyn. Since we were living in Hanover, Anne-Marie went to live with Marilyn at my mom's in Hingham, as it was closer to the school and made their commute easier. In 1982, after graduating, they both came to do a partial apprenticeship at my salon in Hanover.

While working with me, Marilyn and I purchased a Bermuda timeshare unit from a salon client. Before Marilyn married, she backed out of the timeshare and I assumed ownership.

They both left my salon to work elsewhere. Anne-Marie has gone on to open her own high-end salon in Randolph with her husband, Anthony, who handles the business side. They are extremely successful and have had to expand at least twice. You go, Girl!

One of my clients with whom I had become friendly became instrumental in starting me on a life-changing journey by asking me if I was right with God. I wasn't. If she only knew the journey that was to ensue. Thank you, Alice.

So many things happened and one of them was when I met Shirley at the support group. She invited me to a Catholic prayer meeting where I heard the gift of tongues for the first time, and it scared me to the point where I didn't go back. Then Shirley invited me to a Catholic retreat center in Brighton. I went with her. It was there as we were in the chapel that the priest asked us to ask God for what we wanted. I thought about it and could have asked for anything, but simply asked for a hug. God honored that request by enveloping me in His arms immersing me in His love. No one was near me, but I knew it was God.

I left the retreat center knowing God had touched me; but continued to live my life my way, doing whatever I wanted – and it was not Godly - for the next five years. I was meeting my own selfish need of looking for love with the wrong people, in the wrong places, going to clubs, dances, Parents Without Partners, bars, etc. I would be asked to dance and get some attention even if it was a smile or kind word and afterwards leave with the guy. Then, either in their car or at their place, I would let the guy have his way. Of course, this added to my guilt, shame, and fear.

I put myself in many dangerous predicaments with men, making Mary Magdalene look like a saint. After each incident I would go home and try to wash clean, but soap and water cannot clean away inner sin and sin it was. Only the Blood of Jesus can wash away sin and make one clean on the inside, and I had not yet surrendered myself to Jesus.

Somewhere during this period of my life, I attended a ballroom dance with my mother and father. My father asked me to dance, and because my mother was a dance instructor, she had taught him how to lead. When my mother and father danced together, everyone would stop and watch. It was truly beautiful.

With Dad's leading, I was able to follow very smoothly. I did not know how to ballroom dance, but we glided across the floor with ease. This was a very special, precious, and memorable moment for me. Later in the parking lot, my father said he had always wanted to dance with one of his daughters. I am blessed that privilege was mine.

In 1979 on another night out at a singles dance held by Parents Without Partners, I met Roger. Instead of one of my many one-night stands, Roger became my second husband on August 23, 1980. We were married by a Justice of the Peace.

Roger had two children with whom he had visitation every weekend. I would occupy myself while he spent time with them, thinking this was the right thing to do and that I would be in the way. Actually, I was jealous of the time he was spending with them. I wanted his time and attention, never asking Roger what he thought.

I had no idea how to even begin to mesh our two families together and it seemed an insurmountable problem. Instead of trying to figure out how to resolve the issue, I dissolved into self-pity.

Friend Shirley was still in my life and encouraged me to attend church with her. I attended her church in Hingham and later

Roger joined me. Though we attended, Roger and I struggled in our relationship.

I was a very guilt-driven, angry woman. We went to a Marriage Encounter weekend; but nothing helped or changed what was going on between Roger and me.

Shirley invited me to a Billy Graham Crusade in the spring of 1982 in Boston. My daughter and I went with Shirley in a church group on a bus. We responded to the altar call to receive salvation. We said the words, but in hindsight the words alone are not enough. However, this was another step in my journey to get right with God. Anne-Marie and I walked to the front of the stadium where both of us had a different counselor but both from Hanover. The fact that of all the hundreds of people who came forward, our two counselors were from our town was obviously God. Now, little insights about who God was and how He worked were beginning to take hold in me.

God used Shirley mightily in my journey. She persisted with me. One thing changed with me at that time. I had an insatiable hunger for the Bible. I, who never read anything I didn't have to read, was now devouring the Bible. I had almost no understanding of its content, but I was reading it.

I attended a Christian women's group that sponsored a retreat. At that retreat, God began to heal me of the anger I had stored up against my father. This group also had Bible study booklets that I began using. I had no understanding. All this time I was thinking I was okay, and a Christian to boot; after all, I owned my own home and business. What a mess!

One day my father dropped by my salon, which was totally out of character for him and noticed that something was not right with me. So, he asked. I mentioned that Roger and I were struggling in our marriage relationship. When he stopped by, I knew deep down in my heart that because Dad had stopped drinking and he was changing, that he loved me and cared about my life. Thank you, Dad. Thank You, Jesus.

Because I thought I was okay, now having Jesus (which I really didn't), when I arrived home after the Crusade, I asked Roger to leave because in my twisted thinking I didn't need a man now. Men had only hurt and used me. But as I had allowed it to happen this was totally wrong thinking on my part and indicative of my warped thinking. So, Roger went to live in the camper we had recently purchased, which was parked at Ellis Haven Campground.

I was still a very angry woman, but God was not giving up on me and continued working in me. The mess was of my own making, and though with one hand I was reaching for God, the other was still holding onto whatever Miss Maureen wanted. Therefore, nothing changed.

I continued going to church, to a Christian women's group, to Bible Study in Braintree, and once even to a prayer meeting in Dorchester with Shirley.

When we arrived at the Dorchester prayer meeting and parked the car, we were the only two white people in sight. I don't know about Shirley, but I was afraid. And right there, sitting in the car, God put on my heart that there is no color in the Spirit, so I could get out of the car and go into the prayer meeting with Shirley. We did.

I could sense these people really loved God. Though their service was different, it was real. Because I was following Shirley and she never asked me to go again, I didn't return. But I thank God for giving me the knowledge and the love for all people of all races while sitting in that car that night.

I also thank God He didn't give up on me, for He had a special plan for my life as He does for each one of us. Ephesians 2:10, "For we are His workmanship, created in Christ Jesus unto good works, which God hath before ordained that we should walk in them."

I attended a Life in the Spirit Seminar at St Mary's Catholic church at Shirley's request. This was a seven-week seminar. On the night of the praying for the infilling of the Holy Spirit, Anne-Marie showed up at home asking if where I was going had something to do with God. When I said, "Yes," she asked if she could come with me. She had been living with Marilyn at my mother's house.

We went together to the seminar. When the altar call came for those who wanted the infilling of the Holy Spirit, and any family member in attendance was welcome to come, she joined me at the altar. We embraced and cried together.

I did not receive the Holy Spirit at that time, but Anne-Marie said she did with the evidence of speaking in tongues. Our relationship had been strained, and it became better after that night.

Even though something in me still would not surrender, God kept working.

Shirley and some of her family needed a place to live, so I thought it would be a good Christian thing to let them move into my house in Hanover, as Roger was living in our camper in Carver. When I allowed this, darkness entered my home and I knew something was wrong, but didn't understand how or why.

What I know now is that the small bad choices I was making every day kept all God had for me at bay and I was opening the door for larger bad choices, giving Satan liberty in my life.

This didn't just happen. It had been going on for years because of my choices. Having Shirley and some of her family move in was a bad choice but became part of my learning experience.

There were many Christians trying to get through to me. One of them, a prominent Christian leader in our area who knew Roger, came to my home alone to talk with me about reconciling. This man had also made a bad choice. The smell of alcohol on his breath was so strong I became angry that he would come to my home in that condition to talk about Jesus and reprimand me when he obviously also needed reprimanding. Not only had he been drinking, but he also came alone knowing my husband and I had separated. I was the only one home. I could still sense the darkness looming in my home.

One thing he said, however, did stay in my mind and frightened me. That thing was I would lose any anointing if I persisted in this separation with Roger. Something, somewhere in me knew this was truth.

I was learning that just because a person says, "I am a Christian," doesn't mean they make right choices. I also have learned that God will use anybody in any circumstance. And that night God used even that man.

All along this journey God was allowing me to see why I didn't give anyone real place in my life. I didn't trust anyone. As I sit here all these years later typing, it occurs to me that my lack of trust for people overflowed onto God. I was doing the human thing of putting human traits onto God; but God knew that and was patiently waiting as His Plan for my life was unfolding.

On another occasion Barbi also spoke to me about my separation, encouraging me to do the right thing. I listened to all of this information.

I still had a lot of life experiences to live through. I had to see that all of my relationships were based on sex or physical pleasure and not true love. Since God is true love, then there must be false love. My way. What I called love was purely selfish and self-centered and not love at all, but lust. And lust was telling me that my life was all about me.

Shirley and her daughter, along with Ethel, Anne-Marie, and I, planned a trip to my Bermuda timeshare for August 14, 1982. Before we left, Shirley and I attended a home Bible study in Braintree where I first met a whole new group of Christian women.

I arrived there with a red and purple outfit on (short skirt and tights), blonde hair, and long red feather earrings. Years later I was privy to the information that the girls at the study commented to God and each other that He had His work cut out with me. They prayed that I would have a Gethsemane experience. I didn't know what that meant but was soon to find out. It meant that I would come to the place where I would want God's will more than my own and would say as Jesus said in Luke 22:42b, "...nevertheless, not My will but Thy will be done."

Our plane indeed landed in Bermuda on Saturday, August 14, 1982. Shirley asked me to go to church on Sunday morning with her. I agreed but only if she called and found out the details. She didn't and instead ordered a taxi, asking the driver to take us to a Holy Ghost filled church. He drove us downtown to Court Street in Hamilton, but church wasn't for another two hours and the streets were bare, with nothing opened. With my yet unregenerated attitude I chose to go back to the timeshare unit with its air conditioning. It was very hot, and I wasn't going to hang out in the heat.

Shirley came back after church very uplifted with information regarding a revival tent meeting on Thursday, August 19th. This was being held not very far from the hill where our Hamiltonian timeshare stood. Not wanting to commit, I kept putting her off with no answer until after Wednesday night when I went out with Ethel to a bar. I left with some man from the States. I was obviously still living in Maureen-mode, but God used this to show me where I was and that something was still desperately missing in my walk with Him. Seeing myself for who I really was made me willing to go to the tent meeting the next night.

Shirley had become friends with the Hamiltonian timeshare caretaker, Peter. So Shirley, Peter, Ethel, and I went to the revival. The tent meeting had at least 500 black people and we were the only four whites in attendance. Remember, God had done a work in me months before at that prayer meeting in Dorchester. So, it didn't matter what color anybody was.

A minister from New York stood to preach and he started weeping and had to sit down. At that point the entire congregation stood and started praising the Lord. The minister stood again, wept again, and had to sit again. The entire congregation stood again and praised the Lord. On the third attempt the minister preached and what I heard was that if there was anyone out there unsure of their salvation to come forward to the altar. I stood and thought, *At that Billy Graham Crusade I had gone forward because somehow in my mis-wired brain my going forward would encourage Anne-Marie to go forward.* Now here I was with bleached blonde hair, a white dress, and practically the only white person in a crowd of black people on fire for Jesus. This time and quite deliberately, I walked to the front for my sin-sick self. By this time Peter and Ethel had left. Shirley and I stayed.

I had no idea what was about to take place in my life. Everyone was praising and praying. Before I knew what was happening, strange language was pouring out of my mouth. I had been infiltrated by God and by a heavenly language that wouldn't stop for what seemed a long time.

Nobody touched me, but I fell backwards onto the ground. God was about to do a deep work. I could feel my hands being stretched out and pinned down as if nailed on a cross. My feet also were nailed. I was able to speak and move my head but could not get up. I was fighting it for a while and then a worker at the tent meeting spoke softly in my ear saying, "You have to give it all up, Sister."

I experienced going through a long dark tunnel and saw a bright white light and I knew I was going someplace beautiful. I didn't want to come back to earth as I had made and was making such a mess out of my life. After about an hour (I later learned) I heard a worker saying, "Do you want to get up now, Sister?" I got up and Shirley said that I looked like a light bulb all glowing. I stood there swiping my brow and not quite understanding what had just happened to me.

Now I knew the missing element had been the indwelt Godhead. Wanting to be good, knowing that God was the answer, even saying the right words was not enough. Saying the right words does not move God. God reads hearts. God tells us in His Word that we honor Him with our lips, but our hearts are far from Him. That night in Bermuda He knew I was giving Him my heart. He honored it and gave me His. August 19, 1982, I was born again of the Spirit of God. Hallelujah!

What counseling and therapy did not do and could not do to keep me from looking for love in all the wrong people, places, and things, God did during that wonderful and amazing time with Him in the Spirit on the ground in Bermuda.

I was now clean on the inside. This was the beginning of a whole new life: learning how to walk with God in the Spirit rather than fulfilling the lusts of my flesh. Lust is not love. God ***IS*** Love.

That night when Peter returned to the tent meeting, he took Shirley and me out to eat. The bartender was a man we had all met at a different club. I was so excited at what I had just experienced that I shared it with him.

The next day Ethel and I went to the beach. When I shared what had happened to me the night before, she expressed concern that it was probably a cult. I told her I knew what had happened to me was real. And it was. And it is.

That night Ethel, Anne-Marie, Shirley's daughter, and I went to the timeshare's comic show. Every joke was off color and surprisingly offended me; but I stayed. The four of us left in a taxi to go to the disco downtown. Ethel and I went downstairs where the older crowd was. The two girls went upstairs where the younger crowd gathered.

When we entered the disco club, we had to walk through the whole place to get to the bar. When I turned around and looked onto the dance floor, I didn't see people. I saw lusting and luring demons dancing where the people should have been. God had opened my eyes into the spirit realm and it shocked and scared me to the point where I left and never returned. I not only saw the demons but I also heard the Lord Jesus speak telling me to leave for I no longer belonged there.

I told the others I was leaving and then went outside. The bouncer was also outside and since he was someone we had met, I knew him. I believe he saw that something was different with me.

There was a line waiting for a taxi. He asked me if I wanted a taxi and when I told him I did, he took me right up front to the next taxi while others waiting were complaining. He told those waiting that this taxi was for the lady – me, a LADY! Imagine! He knew the taxi driver and asked him to bring me back to the Hamiltonian. He paid the driver to do so. WOW!

I arrived back at the room and started packing for our trip home the next day. I knew because I knew that I had to go back with my husband, Roger.

Before I continue, I have to say a word about the way I dressed up to this point. It was purposefully seductive and alluring, giving a definite message. Regardless of what manufacturers and designers of women's clothes produce, it is my responsibility to dress modestly. I am a woman. God made me female. My heart determines the way I dress. From this point in my life there would be no more low-cut tops, short shorts, or mini-skirts.

When we arrived home that Saturday, I was getting ready to drive from Hanover to our campsite in Carver where Roger and young Donnie were, as Donnie stayed with Roger while I was away in Bermuda.

Shirley and some of her family prayed with me. I told them they can pray but I had decided that I was going.

It was around 10:30 at night when I started to drive. I began to doubt but prayed for God to keep me going in this direction if He wanted me to and He did. I arrived at our camper and Roger was pleasantly surprised to see me. I shared with him all that happened at the tent meeting in Bermuda. We forgave each other and reconciled. God had changed me and taken away the anger inside.

The next day was Sunday and Roger, Donnie, and I went to church. It was obvious that something had changed with us, especially with me. Later that day we went to the church picnic. A friend, Anne Arnold, led my 10-year-old Donnie to accept the Lord, and the three of us were water baptized at a pond in Rockland by our pastor that day. I was very excited and happy because I felt God was fixing my messed-up relationships.

We now had to ask Shirley and her family to find another place to live. God's order was in the process of being restored in my home.

On June 15, 1984, as I was working at my salon, I received a call from my sister, Melanie, that my father had suffered a heart attack and died while working out in the yard at home in Hingham. My heart sank to the floor. My body became weak and I felt as if I would pass out. I am so grateful to God for setting me free from the anger and hate I had towards my father before he died. Because I have zero recollection of his wake and funeral, I know my emotions shut down rather than deal with the pain of losing my Dad I had come to believe really did love me, and whom I loved.

Roger and I attended church regularly. He also joined a Full Gospel Men's Fellowship. Part of that Fellowship was an open breakfast meeting once a month, and Roger and I faithfully attended. Roger became more involved. I met several other Christian women, wives of the men in this Fellowship, many of whom became friends. At this fellowship, Roger met a man involved in a ministry that acted as liaison between the needy and those able to meet their need.

Roger told me he felt God leading him to join this man in ministry. He started out helping in Lowell until an abandoned foundry in Elmira, New York, was given to this ministry. Roger and I agreed to join this man in New York. The ministry included a food pantry and thrift store.

We sold our home in Hanover to my sister, Melanie, and her husband. This was in the summer of 1989.

In the interim, another family also a part of the fellowship kindly allowed us to stay with them in Wollaston.

We had given away everything in preparation for the move.

Five years prior, my mother had suffered a heart attack, had a five-by-pass heart surgery, then suffered a stroke and was confined to a wheelchair. My sisters and I shared taking care of her. Mom sold her house to my sister, Marilyn, and wanted to go to Disney. She invited and paid for my sister, Melanie, and her two children and me to take her. It was a special trip for all of us. So now in November of 1989 she was having some blockage and taken to South Shore Hospital. Her doctor told us she needed constant care and recommended a nursing home. My sisters and I agreed. It was a very hard and emotional decision for us. I was having a hard time with the move to Elmira as Mom was ill in a nursing home in Weymouth. On January 3, 1990, Roger drove me from Wollaston to Weymouth to visit Mom at the nursing home. She was coherent and our visit was joyful, leaving me with another precious memory. The next day she was taken to Carney Hospital after suffering another heart attack, and she died. I remember at her wake that she didn't have her glasses on, and we had to locate them before we would start because we knew her with glasses. They were located and placed on her in the casket. I miss you, Mom.

To accommodate living quarters for Elmira, Roger and I purchased a conversion bus. It needed work to make it livable; but Roger felt he was more than able to do the work necessary and suggested I go to the timeshare in Bermuda while he did so. Off to Bermuda I went.

Roger had been to the foundry before we moved and realized much work was needed. Because of this the man we went to help, who was the head of this ministry, had Roger so busy cleaning and repairing the foundry that little time was left for the bus. What time he did have would only produce more underlying problems. There was no place ready to set up home in Elmira so Roger suggested I stay on in Bermuda, knowing that a previously met friend would welcome me into her home when the timeshare availability was up.

Valerie indeed did welcome me, and I stayed with her for five and a half weeks. She and I are kindred spirits and during those weeks, she and her black community welcomed me with open arms. We had prayer meetings, attended church together, I learned to make a pill box type of hat and in general, we were family. I joined Valerie in her visit to the men's prison where she was to minister. Once inside, she announced to the men that Sister Maureen was going to share. Since there was no time for a heart attack, I stood and shared what God had done in the tent revival meeting. I was expecting to faint when I finished but instead was surprised at the joy that filled me.

I wanted to stay with Valerie and my new-found family in Bermuda. Visa problems, a waiting husband, and God's plan for my life said otherwise.

I arrived back in Massachusetts and stayed with Melanie for a short time until I left for Elmira.

When I arrived in Elmira, the motor coach was not livable, so Roger and I made a two-room space to sleep and eat in on the second floor of the foundry building. The only bathroom on this floor was a men's bathroom with a urinal for both of us to use unless I wanted to go down two large flights of stairs alone in the dark at night. I did not opt to use the stairs. The washer and dryer were also down two flights along with the shower. We had to use the downstairs facilities before 8 A.M. because the ministry doors would then be open. I really did try to make this work. I wanted to please God.

Roger was kept busy all the time and we hardly saw one another. The man in charge of the ministry was to train me in the office but when I would arrive at the office, he would have done everything. I felt less and less needed or useful at this ministry. I would help in the separating of clothing donated and food distribution to those in need. We were ordered after a time to tell the ones coming for help they had to volunteer in order to receive food. I chose not to do that for freely we were given the food through donations to give to those who had need. I was beginning to sense that something was very wrong.

The man in charge had married and he and his wife rented a house. They had it professionally cleaned and nicely furnished. I was jealous and angry and felt sorry for myself and Roger.

Problems with the ministry continued and when I tried to address them at our business meetings, the meetings were ended. Something was very wrong.

Friends came to visit from Massachusetts. During a ministry time of prayer where they joined us, the director openly prayed against my rebellion. I left the circle very upset as I did not consider my speaking the truth a rebellious act.

I resented that I had to live in the messy, dirty foundry on the second floor. I resented the fact that Roger did the majority of the work while the director and his wife lived in luxury compared to our foundry space. I resented that Roger was not given his due. I resented that he and I had given up everything and were now being used. It was becoming obvious to me that this "ministry" was not what it was intended to be. I was helpless as Roger still trusted the director and God was working in me still showing me my sinful heart.

After three months, I planned a trip back to Massachusetts fully determined I wasn't returning to New York. I had said to God that I would go anywhere and do anything, but I was wrong. When I arrived back in Massachusetts, a friend encouraged me that God was at work and I should consider going back. I wanted to punch his lights out, but I did go back.

When I arrived back in Elmira, we rented a small house outside the foundry property furnished with donations received at the ministry. Roger and I were together but not in ministry. He stayed with the ministry. I went back to hairdressing at an adult care home and volunteered at the Crisis Pregnancy Center in town.

Because the motor coach was in need of much repair, the rental of a house seemed a good idea. We moved into a rental house, but Roger would not ask for a raise to help defer the cost of the rental. We struggled financially. The motor coach was sucking up our finances.

Roger found a church he thought I would enjoy, as he and the director were visiting area churches sharing the vision for the ministry. I did attend as he suggested, and he was right.

This church was a lifesaver for me. I worked in the office at the church and became involved with the worship team using banners, flags, tambourines, sign language, and dance. The dance team would go to different churches and teach praise and worship with signing (for the deaf) and dance. We did a routine at the mall at Christmas time. We also did a production on New Year's Eve.

A group from our church went out to the streets to share the gospel. I loved it and was in my element. All of what happened in Elmira was not wasted as I learned much, especially that just because somebody says, "I am a Christian." doesn't mean they are not flawed. All of what happened had been a growth experience for me.

By this time Roger had left the ministry. It was not at all the vision presented to him. Whatever it was, the Spirit of God was not in it. When Roger left the ministry, he obtained a bus driver's license and drove for many senior tours. I was able to join him on a couple of them.

One of the volunteers from the ministry offered us an apartment in a house her son owned. It was on the second floor, and Roger paid the rent by doing odd jobs for the owner of the house, as it was in need of repair.

Because of shady dealings at the ministry, our time there left us with tax debt we could not pay, along with interest and penalties increasing.

I was an angry camper to say it mildly. One night I was shaking Roger and telling him he was not to die and leave me with this debt. I had no idea what was coming when I said this.

Roger's mother sent us some information on a person who gave tax debt help and that person was right in Elmira. We went to her, did all the paperwork, and we waited. We went to the IRS office and spoke with a man there. He said he would have to put a lien on the second mortgage note we held on our Hanover home. When my sister sold the house, they would take that money towards repayment of the debt. I knew that my sister was selling. I was screaming angry and in a rage with Roger, and also with the ministry for not doing the books properly. Roger never communicated any of our concerns with the director. I often thought I should have stepped in, but unfairly expected Roger to do something that was just not in his nature. He would just keep giving demanding nothing in return. This is how he really was.

We never know what is in a day. It is our choice to get right with God and live our life to glorify Him in what we say, think, and do and we still make mistakes. It is a process and can take many years to accomplish. We will not ever be perfect but hopefully we grow as we go along the journey. It is a walk. The word "walk" means to move ahead at a moderate pace.

I was invited to a puppet convention in Tennessee. The couple who invited me was involved with the ministry, so I knew them. In fact, the woman of that couple had previously taught me how to make puppets, and I had already made two of them with her. I decided to go to the convention with them in hopes that it would be used as an outreach for the ministry in Elmira.

Before I left for the convention, I received a check in the mail in the amount of the second mortgage, as my sister had sold the house in Hanover. I wasn't supposed to receive any money. I was under the impression that the IRS was supposed to have put a lien on the Hanover house and receive the money after the sale. That check felt like a hot potato in my hand.

We spoke with a lawyer and he told us to deposit the money out of state. We did and then went back to the IRS to explain what happened. The agent said he could find the money if he wanted to, but he pushed his chair back and replied that he had forgotten to put the lien on the house. The money was mine. I explained that we owed the tax debt and wanted to make it right. He reduced the amount to $10,000 on a $54,000 debt and then reduced it again to $8,000 if we came back that day to pay it. We went right to the bank and withdrew a check and paid it. Only God! Thank You, God. We also paid off a $6,000 debt owed by Roger in back child support.

Off I went to the puppet convention. While there I received a phone call that my son, Donnie, was in a serious automobile accident. I immediately booked a flight back to Massachusetts, and called my friend, Fran, who picked me up at Logan. Fran also came with me to the hospital. Living in Elmira, being absorbed with what Roger and I were doing, I had not kept up with family relationships, so I totally understood that when I arrived at the hospital I was not welcomed. I later learned that Donnie had been pronounced dead.

Obviously, they were able to revive him. By the time Fran and I arrived, Donnie was in the ICU with many tubes ending in him, giving him life support. He had his spleen removed, nine broken ribs, fractured leg (now with a pin in it), a sutured gash on his scalp – but Donnie was alive.

I am so grateful God spared his life. I am so grateful that Fran came with me because my visit there made it obvious that the mess I had made of my family relationships was still a mess. Fran gave me the moral support I needed, and opened her home to me for the few days I was able to stay with Donnie.

Back to New York, Roger and I moved out of our two-room apartment because that house had been sold. Roger was working driving senior bus tours all the while working for his friend still readying the house that had been sold. We moved into our motor coach in September 1995.

That move was not to be for any length of time. One weekend in October while I was at a dance seminar and Roger was driving a bus tour in another part of New York, I experienced lightheadedness and nausea. I felt as if I was about to pass out.

Later when Roger returned to the motor coach alone, he was unable to breathe when he would lay down. I returned from the dance seminar to the church and had a distinct feeling to go home. I found Roger in total distress. God had allowed me to experience what Roger was going through when I had those earlier symptoms. I put on praise and worship music and tried to get him to go to the emergency room, but to no avail. I finally convinced him to let me call a nurse from our church. She told us to get to the emergency room, which we did. I held his hand and prayed all the way. When we arrived at the ER the hospital worker found almost no pulse, so they took him right in. I then filled out the paperwork. I went in to see him and they were about to take blood, so I left. When I did, I knew I wasn't going to see him again this side of Heaven. By this time there were some members of our church in the waiting room for support.

When Roger died that night, three families generously offered me a place to live. I accepted the invitation from a couple who were deacons at our church.

I was with this couple until my move back to Massachusetts. It was something under two months. Our dear host told my friend and I that he thought we were two crazy women. As he got to know us, he said we were the two most grounded in Christ women he knew in that church. That night I knew, because I knew, I was moving back to Massachusetts. I didn't know when or how, but I knew. I had $2,000 cash, no life insurance, no medical insurance, I owed credit card debt and $11,000 to Massachusetts in back taxes, including interest and penalties on the rise that hadn't been settled. With this over my head, I couldn't get a job. Massachusetts would garnish my wages.

Again, God worked it out. I received a call from our tax lady that Massachusetts would accept $3,000 in full payment of our $11,000 debt. She asked if I had the money. I said no, but I would get it. One friend lent me $2,000 and another gave me $1,000. Certainly, another miracle. Thanks to both those friends and thanks to God.

Members from church helped me load a large truck with my belongings, and a friend from Massachusetts drove it back as I followed him. I stayed with him and his wife in Hanson for a short time, and then moved in with friends in Buzzards Bay.

Before leaving Elmira, I gave the motor coach away to a ministry working against abortion. It seemed the right thing to do.

After Roger died and was cremated, I had a service in Elmira at the church we attended. I agreed with Roger's two children to pass his ashes on to them for a service at Bridgewater State College in Massachusetts. They could, when and if they wanted, spread them in places that were meaningful to them.

Before my final move back to Massachusetts, I made a trip in October of 1995. I drove from Elmira with Roger's ashes in the back seat of our small stretch limo, which was our family car. His ashes were in a container the size of a shoebox.

When I arrived at my friend's home in Buzzards Bay where I was to stay for a few days, Barbi asked, "Where is Roger?" I said, "Out in the car." She asked me to bring him in as it was cold, and I told her that he was dead what did it matter; but brought him in anyway. She wanted to look at his ashes as she hadn't seen any before. As we started to open the box Wim, her husband, came and asked, "What do you have?" Barbi responded, "Roger." Wim was a tall, stout man, and he turned white and stepped backwards, looking as if he would pass out. Barbi and I decided we had better not do this. We didn't; but had a good laugh, which we both needed.

When I left New York for good, I stayed a couple of weeks with my friends in Hanson until moving to Buzzards Bay with Barbi and Wim.

Over the next few months, I wrote letters to all my debtors asking how I could pay the debts. Each agreed to a small amount monthly. I was faithful in sending the amount due. Then, one by one, they all wrote letters of loan forgiveness accepting each debt as paid in full.

I found work as a hairdresser in a salon at Walmart in East Wareham. Within two years, I became debt-free. Miracle upon miracle.

While working at the hair salon, God put on my heart one week to give my whole paycheck to another worker whom I knew was on drugs. I did. My only responsibility was to obey God. God knew what He was doing in her life (and mine). I did not have to know what the outcome would be. I needed only to obey God's leading.

I tried to cooperate with each little nudge from God and went to each of my children (with whom at this time I had no good relationship) to ask forgiveness for rejecting them by not keeping up relationship. Because I did not keep up with each one, I was unaware of what was happening in their lives or how they were doing or even where they were living. I didn't think beyond my own selfish need. WRONG! WRONG! WRONG!

I had been praying for God to restore the family. Now in Massachusetts, I would be the one who would make the first steps to restore the broken and strained relationships. I wrote a letter with a little help from a friend to my daughter and stepdaughter without insinuating any blame or guilt on them, taking responsibility for my own failings. I mailed the letters. Though I never received any reply, since that time the tension was gone from our relationships.

I left Barbi and Wim's and rented a small camper close to the hair salon where I worked. It was the first time in my life that I lived alone.

After a year, for physical reasons, I could no longer work as a hairstylist.

The camper I was renting became untenable and I now had to find another place to live. Barbi worked as a caregiver to a lady named Margaret in Buzzards Bay. There was a small efficiency cottage at the back of Margaret's property. She rented it to me for what I could afford.

From Buzzards Bay each day I would drive one hour to Randolph to watch my daughter work, hopefully helping to restore our relationship. I asked her if she was okay with me sitting and watching her as she worked and she said, "Yes."

I had been widowed for five and a half years now, attending Bible studies and keeping myself right with God. No dating. God led me back into the Catholic church after a 35-year absence. 35 years of confession! I simply said, "I have sinned."

Trust me, I had been in other churches I deemed lively and it took me a while to go back, but I knew that's where God wanted me. I started to attend a Catholic church in Buzzards Bay near where I was living at the time and assisted in a Sunday school class. The students asked for a Bible after God's plan of salvation was presented to them. Of course, each one received a Bible.

I was extremely glad and happy to be in close proximity to my family. Anne and Anthony had given birth to my first grandson, Stefano. I was elated when they asked me to move in with them to care for him, which I immediately did.

The income I was receiving from workmen's comp had stopped. My lawyer had told me to file for Social Security Disability under my Social Security number and Roger's. I did. I was denied under my Social Security number. I would now have to find another place to live, so the timing of their invitation was perfect. I was later approved for Social Security Disability under Roger's Social Security number.

Anne and Anthony generously provided me a car and an allowance along with a cell phone. My time was finished in Buzzards Bay and I was now living with Anne and Anthony, caring for Stefano in Whitman. This was definitely a big kiss from God.

I was living there approximately two years when they began pushing me out into life again. I went to a South Shore Singles dance in Abington alone and told Anne and Anthony that if I came back in 20 minutes not to yell at me.

I went and had fun. I did date one man who was deaf. Anne and Anthony would get the number plate and have each one I would date checked out through a police friend. They then would call me and give me a report while I was on the date. It was this man's birthday and I thought, *How am I going to let him know I know it is his birthday?* I didn't have to worry. He mentioned it in our conversation. I dated him only a few times.

The next man I dated was also checked out, and Anne and Anthony called me reporting that he was 84 years old - unknown to me. I was 56. I did go with him and had a nice dinner, but only that once.

One night as I was watching a video, I fell asleep and when I woke up, the community channel was on. I saw a singles over 40 Catholic group advertisement. I waited for it to scroll around again and wrote the number down and called the next day for information. The man who answered was Michael Lynch (my brother's name). So, I went to a members' meeting with my friend, Ethel, and became involved helping to tell others about upcoming events. At this time, I had no idea that I was about to meet my future husband. I didn't meet him at the new-member meeting, but in a few weeks, there was a Connected Catholics group dinner at the Barnside in Pembroke. I attended alone and introduced myself to the line of men as I walked in. At the end of the night with a few of us left, Joe being one, I asked if he was going out to the back parking lot and would he walk us women out. He said, "Yes." I mentioned a board game night the next Friday in Norwell. He made a face as if uninterested in board games, until I asked if he played cribbage. (Thanks, Dad, for teaching me.) He did. I said I did also, and we could play this board game together. The next Friday came and I went, he went, as did one other lady. The three of us did not get the message that it had been cancelled. God at work! We were allowed into the hall and played three-handed cribbage. I believe Joe let us win. Later I read in his Wentworth yearbook that he was on the cribbage team and very good at it. Now I knew he let us win. After the game, Joe invited us for pizza or a hamburger. I agreed and she declined. Joe and I went and talked for quite a while at Not Your Average Joe's restaurant in Norwell. We talked later in life about why there were two of us ladies that didn't get the cancellation message. He told me that he thought I would not have stayed if it were just the two of us.

He asked me out for the next weekend for dinner and a movie. I said I had plans to go to the South Shore Singles dance, but really I wanted to screen the movie choice to make sure it was appropriate for us to watch together. So, I did with two other ladies from our group. Joe and I made the date for the next Sunday.

When I went to the South Shore Singles dance the night before our date, Joe showed up. He asked me to dance, and while dancing, we both thought we fit and had been waiting all our lives for each other. But neither of us expressed that just yet. He did try to kiss me after our dance as we were walking off the floor, but he missed. He said, "Bad move?" I agreed.

Joe would go outside to smoke. When he returned I would be dancing with someone else. He learned very quickly that if he wanted to dance with me, he would have to stop going out for a cigarette. He did stop going out, and we danced every dance thereafter.

The next night we had dinner and watched the movie that I had screened with two lady friends, "Music of the Heart." I watched, pretending I hadn't seen it. He called me and we saw one another every night thereafter. I eventually told Joe that I had prescreened the movie.

One thing about Joe – he was a gentleman. He opened doors for me, including car doors (even in the driveway), everywhere we went. Once in a while, I'd forget and start to open the door, then, catching myself, I'd quickly shut it. Joe told me if I started opening the door, he would stop. There were times others were in the car and they would tell me to just get out. I didn't but waited for Joe to open the door, letting him treat me as special to him. I wasn't used to this treatment, and it felt so good. When we walked together, we held hands. He was a kind, loving, and very humble man. We did a lot of sharing as we saw each other almost every night. I let Joe know right from the beginning there would be no sex unless or until I married. He honored my request even though it wasn't easy for either of us.

We would park in downtown Whitman to talk and or liceman came to the car window. We shared that I daughter and her husband, and Joe lived with his son sharing uninterrupted time.

• • •

> A critical note: Waiting is special and it can be for you also. Lay the ground rules and wait, wait, wait. Don't be robbed of something precious on your wedding night. Keep yourself pure as a special gift to the one you marry. If you have already failed in this area, begin now. Fresh and clean. With God, it is possible.

• • •

When Joe asked me to marry him, I wasn't sure I wanted a third marriage but knew I would marry again, and to a Catholic. I would have been a foolish woman not to have said, "Yes." I asked him why he wanted to marry me, and he answered that I would teach him more about God; but the truth be known, he taught me about LOVE. He was a man of few words, but his actions spoke mega LOVE.

My daughter wanted to see the ring (what she was saying was "don't hurt my mother"). The ring was being designed and made. We planned a wedding for June 2, 2000, and a honeymoon cruise to Bermuda. The number of our room on the ship was 1030. We had met on October 30th. A little kiss from God telling us we had His approval. We knew that, but God was being His gracious Self. We loved cruising and went on many more to Bermuda out of Boston... totally convenient.

Before we were married, we went to a function where we met Cardinal Law of the Boston diocese of the Catholic church. In conversation I shared with him that Joe and I were getting married, and we had decided that there would be no sex until we were married, as I had been there and done that before and wasn't doing it again. He responded, "I should hope not." HA, HA, HA.

We married and meshed our families together, along with our finances. We were one. We purchased a house in an over-55 East Bridgewater community. Only one person had to be over 55 years old. (That would be me.)

Joe became instant Papa first to Stefano, and then Sofia, who was born six weeks prior to our wedding. Sandro was born two years later when they had moved from Whitman to Easton.

To the glory of God and to our great delight, Scott and Danni married and eventually graced us with more grandchildren, a boy, Robert, and a girl, Devin. In the years since, they purchased and moved into a lovely home in Bridgewater.

While trimming a tree in the first steps of cutting it down, Scott's ladder slipped from under him. He found himself flat on the ground with a compression fracture in his back. After an agonizing recovery, Scott was finally able to return to work. During that time and to her credit, Danni took on extra hours at work to see them financially through. Bravo to both of you.

Donnie and Wendy married and had twin boys, Nathan and Nicholas. Wendy was diagnosed with melanoma. During this time, Donnie stayed home, caring for her and the twins. In my eyes, he was the man of the hour. Wendy died at home when the twins were two and a half. This was heart-breaking for the entire family. However, in God's gracious love, He brought Tanya into Donnie's life. The four of them have become a loving family and were united as such in marriage August 16, 2019.

Joe's younger son and his wife came to us asking our advice regarding adopting a girl from Guatemala, and in need of help with it. We were excited to help. This adoption brought the blessing of Isabella into our lives.

We loved each one of our grandchildren equally as they came along. We loved having them over and watching them grow. Papa was very easy going with them. He would be asleep on the couch and one or more of the grandchildren would pinch his nose or cheek and he just let them. I on the other hand lost it at times mostly because of the noise or whining. Joe would tell me, it's only noise. Forgive me for the times I lost it. What a privilege and a blessing. Joe was a magnet drawing each one in.

Joe's older son has a brilliant mind. He is a professor at the university in Bridgewater. Their conversations were way over my head. I am now learning to ask questions, thus participating in conversations and not of my own making feeling left out.

My first husband, Donnie, was now mostly housebound because of sickness. He lived in Halifax, the next town to where Joe and I lived in East Bridgewater. I would bring the twin boys over to visit him and my husband, Joe, was okay with this. While Donnie visited with the boys, I was talking to his aide and Donnie would stop me, saying that he didn't want to hear about God. I brought him my homemade lasagna and the twin boys to visit a few times.

One day I received a phone call from his aide, saying Donnie said he needed God in his life and to call me. Donnie came to the phone, but for whatever reason our conversation was interrupted. After hanging up, God told me to go to his place to share in person; obviously, God knew Donnie needed a more personal touch. So, I went over and led him to receive Jesus as his Lord and Savior. I could see the change in him. He wasn't just reciting words. Something deep inside had happened to him. The timing was God's. Don died five days later and is now in Heaven. I shared this with all who came to his house that day and some said that it didn't sound like Donnie, but I told them this is what happened. Donnie knew his time was short and that he had a need for God.

Four years later in January of 2017, my Joe had been losing weight without trying. The weight loss continued until it was very noticeable.

Joe's lifelong hobby had been antique tools. He bought and he sold. He went to every auction from Pennsylvania to New Hampshire. There was an auction coming up in New Hampshire and he did not want to go to the doctor until after that auction at the end of April. He was so weak and though I was worried about his going, I knew I had to let him go. It was the last auction he went to and God was with us both.

I had a trip planned for May with my friend, Ethel. Joe insisted we go. All along I knew I wasn't going, but I let him think I was because he would insist I go.

He went to the doctor on May 3rd and was diagnosed with stage 4 liver cancer. It started in the gall bladder and was choking his liver. He became weaker and weaker and chemo was an option; but he became so weak that he wasn't strong enough for the chemo.

I took care of Joe at home. When I could no longer care for him, I had hospice come in as suggested by the doctor. Hospice was there for only three days before Joe died peacefully at home surrounded by his loving meshed family and friends. Joe was the love of my life and it was a devastating loss to have him die. I miss you, Joe, so very much.

The first piece of jewelry Joe bought me was a birthstone ring that I had misplaced for many years. After Joe died, I was cleaning out a plastic bin in the linen closet and there at the bottom of the bin was the ring. God gave me a special memory of my Joe. Joe kept telling me it would turn and not to worry. This was his favorite saying whenever I would lose or misplace something.

I knew that I would not stay in our house and put the house on the market. The house sold to the first looker, and at asking price. I asked if we could wait until September to sign papers as I was overwhelmed with decisions on how to handle closing down the house. The buyers were willing to wait. There was so much to clean out, and I needed the summer to take care of business. I knew I was to move in with Anne and Anthony and their family as they had opened their home to me. I moved in with them in the middle of September 2017, for the next chapter of my life.

Part Two

Life at Masciarelli's

And so life begins at the Masciarelli's: My Anne-Marie and Anthony with their three children: Stefano, Sofia, and Sandro, and their two dogs.

How foolish it would be of them or of myself to think that my coming here was simply a haven for an old widow. The gifts they have given me in the love and security of being part of a family is more than a blessing as one grows older. Above and beyond, even that is the blessing from my heavenly Father of continuing the good work He had begun in me of revealing the hidden things that were keeping me in a self-made prison. He has used instance after instance of being with this dear family to continue to grow me up and set me free. I can feel myself more and more entering into His promise of Sabbath Rest (that Place spoken of in Hebrews 4:9-10 that tells us when we have stopped doing things our own way and come to follow God's leading, we enter His Place of Rest).

The first day I arrived, Sandro came home from school and thanked me for being there. After being in a quagmire of emotions from Joe's illness, Joe's death, knowing I couldn't stay in the house, sorting through everything to decide what was to be given away and what was to be brought to Anne's, to seeing Joe's precious tools being removed from the basement to be auctioned and entering into a new chapter of life, Sandro will never know how deeply his words touched me. I felt welcomed. I felt at home. And I knew I was where God really wanted me to be. Even thinking about it now makes me realize how blessed I am that God is restoring my soul. For so long

I had shut off my ability to acknowledge or even want to be able to experience my heart's feelings with anyone but Joe and one trusted friend. Now I could freely express how blessed and glad I was for Sandro's thanking me for being there.

Many other little daily circumstances with my grandchildren have also encouraged me.

For example, the boys wanted ferrets. FERRETS! Help, God. They are rodents. But the boys wanted the rodents. I tried, but I couldn't help freaking out when one of the rodents found its way into my room. Boys being boys, they thought this was great sport. Sooooooo come to find out the father actually paid the son to freak out the nana. As I was at my computer, I felt something moving around my feet. I jumped up and screamed, "Someone get this ferret out of my room!" Sandro came and took it away. Whereupon I immediately went to his room and accused him loudly. Then I noticed Anthony in the hallway chuckling as he was obviously enjoying the scenario.

You don't play games like that with people you don't love. God even used that ferret to show me I was loved and welcomed. It has not made me love ferrets; it has surely deepened my love for my family.

Now let me tell you about Sofia. Sofia was turning the magic 18. She had decided on an all-girls dinner out in Boston for her birthday. Anne surprised her by ordering a limo as the magic chariot ride. But for me, her invitation was the real surprise. Sofia specifically invited me to come to be a part of her celebration. I was the only old lady there and enjoyed every minute knowing my granddaughter wanted me there.

Just as special is the fact that when Sofia is home, she and her boyfriend play cards with me. They know it is something special to me, and they make me feel special by joining me in it.

My firstborn grandson, Stefano, and I, through circumstances that don't matter here, have developed a camaraderie as we drive back and forth to his place of employment every day. The hours we spend in the car have given me an inroad into Stefano's heart and mind that would never have been talked about any other way. And for that I thank God and I thank Stefano. On occasion we even stop for dinner on the way home. One of those times provided Stefano with a new experience. He got to shuck his lobster for the first time. It was fun for both of us.

While living with Anne and her family I am once again in awe of my daughter. Her business acumen as she partners with her husband is more than to be applauded and often blows me out of the water.

In the 36 years I've known Jesus, one of the most precious aspects of His character He has revealed to me is that of Healer. When I became born again, my spirit was healed. The Triune Godhead inhabited my spirit. Nothing can ever change that, and nothing can be more whole than that. God often touches peoples' bodies and blesses them with a physical healing. When that happens, we call it a miracle. We call it a miracle because it is not the norm. Our bodies were made from dust and they will return to dust. We don't need them in heaven because we will have new immortal bodies. What remains then is our soul. The soul is what makes us us. It is where we think, reason, choose, and emote. Most of the Bible is written for the benefit of our soul. When I speak of the precious aspect of Jesus as Healer this is the area I am addressing.

When I speak of the soul, I mean the mind, the will, and the emotions. I quote a friend with this explanation of the soul: If you were in an accident (God forbid) and found yourself lying in a hospital bed unable to speak, unable to hear, unable to see, unable to move, you would still be there hidden inside your body. You would be unable to communicate but you are there. That you is your soul.

For 36 years Jesus has been working in my soul. Because it is imperative that we come to understand the way God works, I will share some of the things He has done. As you read you will understand why it is easy to attribute God's working in my life to mere human emotions or even emotional or mental illness. I realize this is a sensitive area, but that does not change truth.

As I share the instances that have happened here and that God used, please remember the mountain of guilt and anger and fear that had been built up over the last 70-odd-years. It took several months to understand and realize that God was exposing deep, hidden things in me, using my learning to live in a new and different family environment, in order that those hidden things could no longer hold me prisoner. I think this is a good place to stress the importance of learning to have a close personal relationship with God. It doesn't happen overnight. Like any relationship, it takes time. But if I had not spent the majority of my Christian experience learning how to walk with God, I would not be able to see so clearly how He has used my being here with this wonderful family to remove those vice grips on my heart. So very often in the process when fear would grip me, I had to force myself to remember that God brought me here. Habitual walking with Him had taught me that since He brought me here there was reason. Each time I asked Him the reason, He gave me a flashback of an instance from my youth that had been buried. Each instance had to be dealt with individually and completely before healing would come.

For example, one night I was awakened by what was to me intense fierce yelling. My heart was pounding, paralyzing me with fear. I got up, and sitting on the edge of my bed, began praying. I continued to pray, and things quieted down. I know that my reaction was an over-reaction and that something in me needed healing. The Holy Spirit revealed one source when as a child there was a loud noise from outside my bedroom to which I reacted in fear. When God revealed that instance to me, I could deal with it. As a 73-year-old woman, I now knew what that loud noise was. I sat there with the Holy Spirit and forgave those involved from my childhood and thanked God for those involved now for using them to make me whole. Had I chosen to stay in bed and pull the covers over my head, healing would not have come.

As an adult I have learned when I have an over-reaction, I know that something needs healing in me. I need to realize it, face it, and deal with it. Jesus is the Healer and He knows the perfect time as He does all things well. If I try to delve into my past on my own, I may do untold damage and spend a lot of money on counselors who cannot read my heart. Only God knows my heart and what is needed for healing in His timing and in His way.

As I proofread this, it occurs to me how very gracious God was in letting me just enjoy my time with Joe before beginning His work in this freeing but traumatic experience of healing. God's timing is essential and perfect. Life with Joe was God's gift of a 17-year parentheses for which I will ever be grateful.

Let's continue. Sofia is great at getting up in the morning. The boys are not. In order to give them a Nana-help, I set my alarm to go in and wake them up. I am glad to be able to contribute to helping smooth their morning.

Because of the two instances regarding my brothers where undue responsibility had been laid on my doorstep, I had developed the habit of both shirking and being angry when given responsibility. Every person in a family needs rightly to take and live up to responsibility. It did not take long for God to reveal this other area where I needed healing.

As God allowed me to be put in situations demanding responsibility, He taught me about the communication necessary to accompany the responsibility. I am learning how to relate with my beloved grandchildren who are now young adults. I am gaining a healthy respect for my daughter and son-in-law who manage two businesses, do their best at raising their independent offspring, and keep up with an active social life, all the while maintaining some semblance of order in their very peopled home life. I embrace the opportunity to help where I can and to enjoy being with those I love.

At one point, Stefano was unable to drive. One consequence was that he now had no way to get to his job, an hour from the house. Because their business was in an opposite direction from Stefano's job, I offered to drive him at least the first day. After I dropped him off, I asked the Lord in total self-pity why I had to pay the price for Stefano's sin. Instantly came the words that He had paid the price for my sin and what if driving Stefano was all He wanted me to do for now. I got the message.

As with all things God does, driving Stefano to and from work this past year has been one of the most rewarding experiences of my life. It has deepened our relationship and enabled me to share life on a gut level with him that under different circumstances would not have been possible. When the courts decide to give Stefano back his license, I will miss our time together.

This new family life is wonderful, and I appreciate it even though at times I really miss my Joe. One day while alone driving in my car, listening to the Christian song "The Power of Your Love," I became weepy missing him. I asked God about what was happening because I knew if I was feeling sorry for myself that was not a good place to be. The car then became filled with the presence of God enveloping me in His Love. It was very gentle and at the same time very powerful. I was immersed in His presence. There is not an experience on this earth or words that could have described what happened. God was telling me Joe is not with me here, but He is and would give me what I need when I need it… and He knew I needed that saturation of His Love.

Later that day when I arrived at Sandro's school to pick him up, I was composed enough to share my experience with him. On the ride home his response was an amazed, "Really?" That evening I had the opportunity to share it with Sofia. Her response was, "WOW!" For the next week or so I couldn't stop telling people what God had done for me.

In early March, Anne and Anthony left for Miami on a scheduled business trip. While they were away, the forecasted winter storm accelerated into the worst blizzard New England had in years. Thank God they had the foresight to hook the generator up before they left. The kids and I managed to keep things going all through the storm. Once again, I could feel the anxiety of over-reacting to situations where I was responsible. God was still showing me the need of much healing. I also thank God and Anne and Anthony for asking a neighbor to keep check on us (which they did).

During the storm, one of Sandro's friends stayed with us for the three days. Once again, my rebellion at being held responsible reared its ugly head. I thank God that He showed me that and He was dealing with it. I also thank God that during this sequestered time the kids and I had marvelous conversations about life and God. At one point, Sandro mentioned a song he had heard about God having a plan for each life, "Choice, Choice, Choice." My heart rejoiced. Something about God was sinking into Sandro. Anne texted continually to make sure we were okay. My emotions had screamed that this was too much, but God showed me it was a blessing.

When Anne returned home, I was able to share with her about Paul's drowning and why I had balked at taking responsibility, but God was healing me and using her family to do it. One day I will embrace responsibility.

Back to loud noises in the night. I was able to share with Sandro why loud noises day or night cause me to react in fear. I assured him God was working on this area in me. Sometimes when I hug him, he hangs on. I told him that he is a very important young man, and I love him. Bless God!

On one occasion loud noises caused my heart to fiercely pound and again I was paralyzed with fear. I prayed until the noise subsided. The words of the hymn "A Mighty Fortress" were sounding in my mind. The words assured me once again that Jesus within me is greater than anything, including my own emotions that can come against me. Calm returned to my soul. God's work was continuing.

Because these instances kept unearthing panic inside of me, I was praying with one of my friends. During that prayer time, God brought to my mind a terrible argument I had with my dad. Both of us did and said things for which we were sorry. I also remembered a story related on earlier pages of being at a party that ended up in a shooting. Two buried instances brought to the light for God to heal. Through forgiveness and willingness for God to work in me, I was slowly being set free and experiencing the blessed release of that freedom.

One night when Sandro and Stefano were just boys being boys, rough roughhousing, my heart pounded fiercely in fear, but this time when I prayed, the fear subsided quickly. Thank God. I thought if I die, I win, for I will be at home with God in heaven. I got up and anointed myself with oil and used my worship streamer to praise God. Worship streamers have become an integral part of my prayer life and therefore a mighty spiritual weapon. Devils hate to hear us praise God, and they flee from it.

Later that night I heard the train whistle sound (a message alert on my phone) but there was no message on my phone, so I got up again and sat with God, receiving a word from Him that brought peace to my heart. Thank You, Lord.

I would like to add here that the noises occasioned by family life were in no way directed at me yet used by God to bring healing to me. God's ways are not our ways. They are far better.

Being given the opportunity to live with my grandchildren, God has opened many doors in conversation to share why I do what I do and why I don't do what I don't do. A life lived either for Christ or for the way of the world has more power than one would imagine. Therefore, each life matters. What we do really does speak louder than what we say.

Unfortunately, after my Joe died, instances happened that caused strained relationships between our blended families. During a Bible study I realized I had to take the initiative if healing was to occur. "If at first you don't succeed," became my mantra. Being careful not to play the Blame Game (we usually blame others because we judge their motives and that is wrong), I knew I had to persevere. I prayed. I waited. I sent notes. But more importantly, I trusted that God was working. Almost a year later, the breakthrough came. I received a phone call. As an added kiss from heaven that phone call came on my Joe's birthday. With much prayer, restoration was slowly happening.

Through little daily instances I was beginning to see my grandchildren making Godly decisions. I was also seeing myself being more sensitive to my family's needs. So many people are involved. So many needs. Overwhelming for me but not for God. God is at work in each life. I am learning to accept situations even though I may not like them. I am learning to leave them alone, to wait, and trust God.

As the months flew by, living in this wonderful busy household put me in situations where old fears surfaced. Because I had disciplined myself to obey Jesus, these fears that once paralyzed me were now losing their power. Freedom was on the horizon.

On Thursday, June 14, 2018, God impressed upon me to stop watching TV. I was allowing it to rob me of my time, my energy, and therefore, any possibilities that God might have for me. Believe me, there is life beyond TV.

I quickly became aware that for me food, shopping, and TV had become my methods of escape from life. Ephesians 2:10 clearly states that God has a plan for each life. Escape from that plan in any form is rebellion and therefore, sin.

I have been amazed at how full and meaningful life can be when it is faced and lived in cooperation with God, and agreement with His plan.

It takes time and effort to seek and develop the avenues of life that God intends for us. More and more I am learning that it is worth the effort. I am also seeing as I more and more obey God, God more and more opens doors for me to share with my grandchildren the blessings of walking with Him. I am more and more aware that my new way of life is instrumental in breaking habit-patterns formed by those things that once held me prisoner (food, TV, and shopping).

When I came to the Lord, He delivered me from the ungodly sinful activities. Now He was in the process of delivering me from socially acceptable but meaningless, though seemingly less destructive, activities. Because these activities are socially acceptable, they were really more insidious in keeping me from truly walking with God.

For example, I find myself visiting friends and family more often and building relationships during these visits. As a result, I am seeing doors open to share the things of Christ, and miracle of miracles, God has graced me to pray with some of these people as they invite Jesus into their hearts, lives and minds. Oh, Yes! There is life beyond TV and shopping.

In all of this, God was continuing to impress upon me His desire for me to continue sharing Christ crucified, becoming our sin, and giving us His righteousness.

Another thing that was prime during this time was contacting people from my past and asking forgiveness.

I praise God for my room at Anne's. It has become my sanctuary, my garden where I meet with God. But at one point in my mind, my sanctuary turned into a prison. I thought of Paul's writing that he was a prisoner of the Lord. I had this same feeling when I was at the ministry in New York. I was brought to the scriptures where Paul said he was the prisoner of the Lord. I knew God was "fixing" my thinking in this area. Now I know that I am free to choose my prison. Will I allow life circumstances to imprison me or will I choose to be God's prisoner? This really is a no brainer. God's prison brings freedom from the cares of the world. God's prison brings peace of heart and mind. God's prison brings light to my darkness. God's prison means His grace is sufficient whatever life puts before me.

In late 2018, I was in the car listening to a song by Keith Green, "There is a Redeemer." I became weepy and thought of how I could thank God. Just saying the words, "Thank You," didn't seem enough. I then thought that the way to thank Him is by listening to Him and obeying with my actions. Actions really do speak louder than words.

Praying daily on the telephone with a friend for the salvation of our families and for those in the circumference of our lives is an action God has honored, as we see relationships healed and people come to the saving knowledge of the Lord Jesus Christ. By the way, another powerful spiritual weapon is a prayer partner, one who knows how to get into the presence of the Lord and pray His heart and not their own. Why not ask God to bring such a person into your life?

Part Three

Lessons Learned

Thirty-seven years of walking with Jesus. The first several of those years I worked hard trying to do it on my own. All I got was tired. Slowly and painfully I turned the reins over to the Holy Spirit. That's when change happened. That's when I began to learn. It was a battle then. It is a battle now. It will always be a battle. But as I begin to share with you the things I have learned, I can fully attest to the fact that the price of giving up my selfish and self-absorbed lifestyle – every single battle - was more than worth the freedom from the prisons I had made by poor choices and all those wrong decisions; by doing things my way rather than being led by God's Holy Spirit.

My life is not what I expected it to be. From reading Parts One and Two you know God had His hands full; but nothing is too difficult for God. He used His rod and His staff. He used His pruning shears. He even used a giant axe to lop off what needed to be lopped off. And miracle of miracles, I am on Freedom's holy road.

The little quips that fill this Part Three I share because they are constant reminders when I feel myself being pulled back to my old life and old habits.

I need these reminders. I hope they will be of help to you.

You may want to put stickies or little cards where you can see some of them. They really do help.

- My time on this earth is not about me—it is about Jesus.
- Esteeming others and caring for them before I care for myself is essential.

- Give expecting nothing in return. We give to God. We give in God's name. What people do with it is between them and God.
- Never sit idle. There is a time for rest, but even then, we can pray. If it is not rest time and you have nothing to do, find something to do; do it heartily unto Jesus, not man, all the while be sure you are being a blessing to someone.
- Words have power. We can slice a person to pieces, or we can slather them with honey.
- God has a plan for each life. Play the hand dealt to you… don't look at or desire anybody else's hand.
- Whatever happens, take it from God's hand and ask Him how He wants you to deal with it. Whatever the circumstance, God has a reason. Trust Him.
- God chooses what we go through, but we choose how we go through it!
- My sin is my responsibility and evidence of a wrong heart attitude.
- Take labels and expectations that go with those labels off others. Accept them for whom they are. Don't try to change them. Pray for them. Trust and obey God, leaving the results in His hands. It is God's work to do the changing.
- Do not take things personally. Practice instant forgiveness. Practice instant forgiveness. Practice instant forgiveness. In case you didn't get it… practice instant forgiveness.
- Jesus is not the center of my life. He is not the captain of my ship. He is not the pilot of my plane. Jesus IS my life.
- Instead of being like the Wicked Witch of the West complaining that she was melting, rejoice that the old nature feels as if it is melting. But do not deceive yourself. Stop reading your Bible. Stop living 24/7 in your heart and mind with

Jesus. Stop communicating with God. All too soon you will discover your old nature has gone nowhere. Better to keep on keeping on with Jesus letting Him shine through you.

- No Blame Game. I am responsible for my life.
- Do not hibernate mentally when you do not understand a conversation. Listen. Ask questions. You may learn something. More importantly, you will be interacting with the people God has put in your life.
- Give thanks for and in everything. It pleases God when we do this as it shows Him we trust Him and believe in His omniscience.
- God loves a cheerful giver. Give of your time, your energy, your effort, your livelihood, all the while thanking God for giving you the opportunity to bless others.
- Wrong attitudes (resentfulness, anger, frustration,) reveal a wrong heart.
- Life is about RELATIONSHIP with God. Now is all we have. So don't wait.
- Self-pity is Satan's babysitter, free of charge.
- Teens are a marvelous complex confusion. Don't preach. Don't teach. Just HUG.
- Hate the sin but love the sinner.
- Whisper rather than yell.
- In learning spiritual lingo FORGIVENESS takes the cake.
- God is REAL. God is TRUE. God is FAITHFUL.
- God has given us a gift. It is a brain. We need to use it to His glory, or we will be vulnerable to anyone who speaks with authority.
- Life is a battle fought better with the Bible than with a bazooka.
- Don't use Christian clichés—put truth in your own language.
- Don't let things fester. FORGIVE and bless the offender.

- Man reads actions. God reads hearts. Don't confuse the two.
- Jesus overcame the world. I only have to overcome me.
- Cyberspace is surreal. Life with Jesus is SO real.
- Life with Jesus is higher than any addiction can take you.
- Religion is an x-ray. It exposes but cannot change. Relationship with Jesus both exposes and changes.
- Only God can speak to me in a way that makes me know it is Him.
- Jesus doesn't give up on me, so why should I.
- Jesus is my Light in the Darkness.
- When I obey God, I discover that His grace really is sufficient.
- The timetable is God's not mine.
- The three prime ingredients for a life that pleases God are FORGIVENESS and OBEDIENCE and TRUST.
- Jesus came for people, not religion!

Most people have the mindset that only affirmative answers to our prayers are God answering prayers. But God hears and answers every single prayer. Sometimes He answers yes. Sometimes the answer is no. Sometimes the answer is not yet. And sometimes the answer is silence. We need to learn that He is God, He has a Plan, He has a purpose and we need to agree with Him. When He says no, or wait, or is silent is He still God? Best you think about that.

One last word, and most important for you to understand, is that whatever method you choose to rid yourself of yourself and draw yourself closer to Jesus, for you that method has become a spiritual weapon. Keep your quiver full.

Afterword

I have honestly recorded my story to the best of my memory. I am not proud or happy with the way I made decisions in my first 39 years. However, because of the way God has dealt with me and because He is using my past to His glory and to help others, I would not change any of it. I have come to know and to understand the devastation of sin. I have also come to know and experience the wonder of forgiveness. Whatever your circumstance please be encouraged that He can and will do the same for you if you in all honesty cry out to Him.

My prayer is that you will glean truth and desire it in your most hidden places, and you will allow Jesus to bring forgiveness and wholeness into every part of your being.

It has probably taken you an hour or so to read this book. It took two years of slow, painful drudging up buried memories to write, to organize the timeline, to forgive and be forgiven, to breathe.

I could and would not have done it alone. But I have a persistent friend who knew it was God's bidding and God's timing. Our sessions were prayerful, tearful agony for both of us. Without her insisting on my waiting on the Holy Spirit when I did not want to unearth the misery, and without the faithful Holy Spirit, this book would not have seen this conclusion. The fact that it was God at work is testimony to our continued and deepened friendship. With hearts full of praise and thanks we both say, "Amen."

God has a purpose and a Plan for every life, including yours. I have learned that the sooner I cooperate and walk in His purpose and Plan, regardless of life's circumstances, I have the peace of heart and mind Jesus promised. I have joy unspeakable and full of glory deep down in my soul.

That, Dear Reader, is my prayer for you.

In the Love of Jesus,
Maureen Doyle